Who Has Seen the Wind?

Who has seen the wind?
　Neither I nor you:
But when the leaves hang trembling,
　The wind is passing through.

Who has seen the wind?
　Neither you nor I:
But when the trees bow down their heads,
　The wind is passing by.

CHRISTINA ROSSETTI

Who Has Seen the Wind?

An Illustrated Collection of Poetry for Young People

Museum of Fine Arts, Boston

RIZZOLI
NEW YORK

FRONTISPIECE
Meadow with Poplars, about 1875
Oscar Claude Monet (French 1840-1926)
Oil on canvas, 21 1/2 x 25 1/4 inches
Bequest of David P. Kimball in memory of his wife,
Clara Bertram Kimball 23.505

❦

First published in the United States of America in 1991
by Rizzoli International Publications, Inc.,
300 Park Avenue South, New York, N.Y. 10010 and
Museum of Fine Arts, Boston
465 Huntington Avenue, Boston, MA 02115

❦

❦

Who has seen the wind? : an illustrated collection of poetry for young people
Kathryn Sky-Peck : [illustrations from] Museum of Fine Arts, Boston.
p.   cm.   Includes indexes.
Summary: Comprises a collection of thirty-seven well-known poems
illustrated with thirty-five famous paintings.
ISBN 0-8478-1423-8
1. Children's poetry, English. 2. Children's poetry, American.
[Poetry--Collections. 2. Painting.] I. Sky-Peck, Kathryn.
II. Museum of Fine Arts, Boston
PR1175.3.W48 1991   91-10864
821.008'09282--dc20   CIP   AC

EDITED BY Kathryn Sky-Peck
DESIGN BY Nai Y. Chang

PRINTED AND BOUND IN SINGAPORE

REPRINTED 1992

Contents

Who Has Seen the Wind?

Have you ever seen the wind? What does it look like? Does it have a color? Does it have a shape?

I'm sure you've seen curtains fly away from the window, a kite sail in the air, your hair whip away from your face. But it's not really the wind you've seen.

Sometimes the wind is a soft breeze, and you see a tiny red leaf gently dropping down from a tree in autumn. And sometimes the wind is ferocious, and you see a frenzy of waves and whitecaps on the water. Have you seen the wind? Or have you seen the effect of the wind on the world around you?

When we look at a painting of a tree, we see the tree through the eyes and feelings of the artist. A picture of the same tree by another artist would be quite different. That is because we are seeing not only the tree, but how the artist was affected by the tree. We're looking at one instant that has been captured forever.

Poems and paintings are alike in this way. Each one takes a very special moment and freezes it in time. Poetry does it with words and with sound. Poems have an almost musical quality. Paintings bring the world to life with color and brushstrokes. Sometimes we feel we could almost walk into a picture and live there!

Poems and paintings are full of moods and feelings and hopes and dreams. They can make us happy or sad. They can bring back memories. We can use poems and paintings to picture the world as we would like it to be.

Poems and paintings also help us see the world in new and fresh ways. How many times have you passed a meadow of flowers–and not even taken a second look?

Have you ever stopped and looked at it the way Monet must have seen it? Or have you ever "listened" to what the flowers were saying to you? This is what Henry Rago does in his poem, "Childhood Painting Lesson."

In this book we're taking you on a tour of some very well-known paintings and poems. For fun, we've matched poems and paintings together to show you different ways that artists view the world around them. You'll find paintings of dogs and poems about dogs; paintings of fish and a poem about what fish must think about!

Maybe you'll look at these paintings and want to write your own poems. And maybe you'll read these poems and want to paint your own pictures. Most of all, we hope this book will help you "see the wind."

THE EDITOR

Where Did You Come From, Baby Dear?

Where did you come from, baby dear?
Out of the everywhere into here.

Where did you get your eyes so blue?
Out of the sky as I came through.

What makes the light in them sparkle and spin?
Some of the starry spikes left in.

Where did you get that little tear?
I found it waiting when I got here.

What makes your forehead so smooth and high?
A soft hand stroked it as I went by.

What makes your cheek like a warm white rose?
I saw something better than anyone knows.

Whence came that three-cornered smile of bliss?
Three angels gave me at once a kiss.

Where did you get this pearly ear?
God spoke, and it came out to hear.

Where did you get those arms and hands?
Love made itself into hooks and bands.

Feet, whence did you come, darling things?
From the same box as the cherub's wings.

How did they all just come to be you?
God thought about me, so I grew.

But how did you come to us, you dear?
God thought about you, so I am here.

GEORGE MACDONALD

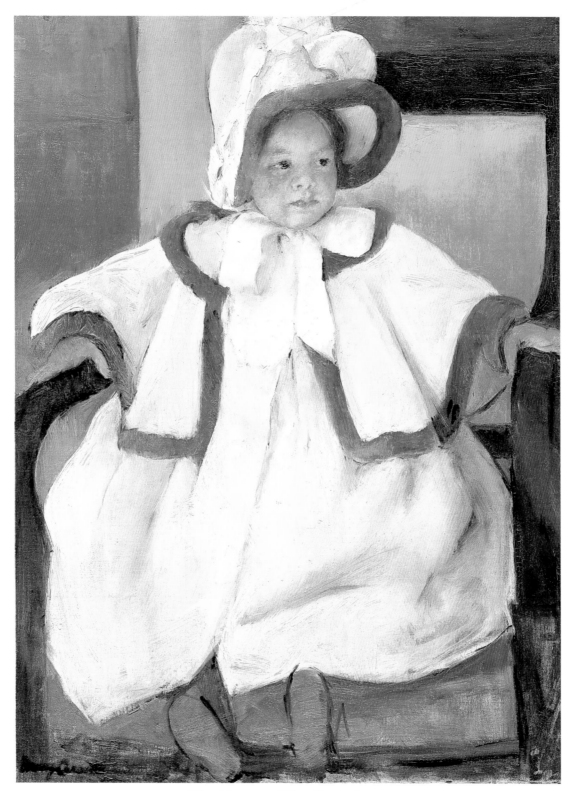

MARY STEVENSON CASSATT: *Ellen Mary in a White Coat*, about 1896

JOHN SINGER SARGENT: *Miss Helen Sears*, 1895

Little Girls

If no one ever marries me,
     And I don't see why they should,
For nurse says I'm not pretty,
     And I'm seldom very good–

If no one ever marries me,
     I shan't mind very much,
I shall buy a squirrel in a cage,
     And a little rabbit hutch;

I shall have a cottage near a wood,
     And a pony all my own,
And a little lamb, quite clean and tame,
     That I can take to town.

And when I'm getting really old–
     At twenty-eight or nine–
I shall find a little orphan girl
     And bring her up as mine.

SIR LAWRENCE ALMA-TADEMA

JACOB MARIS: *Teaching the Dog*

My Dog

His nose is short and scrubby;
    His ears hang rather low;
And he always brings the stick back,
    No matter how far you throw.

He gets spanked rather often
    For things he shouldn't do.
Like lying-on-beds, and barking,
    And eating up shoes when they're new.

He always wants to be going
    Where he isn't supposed to go.
He tracks up the house when it's snowing—
    Oh, puppy, I love you so.

MARCHETTE CHUTE

The Children's Hour

Between the dark and the daylight,
When the night is beginning to lower,
Comes a pause in the day's occupations
That is known as the Children's Hour.

I hear in the chamber above me
The patter of little feet;
The sound of a door that is opened,
And voices soft and sweet.

A sudden rush from the stairway,
A sudden raid from the hall!
By three doors left unguarded
They enter my castle wall!

I have you in my fortress,
And will not let you depart,
But put you down into the dungeons
In the round-tower of my heart.

And there I will keep you forever,
Yes, forever and a day,
Till the wall shall crumble to ruin
And molder in dust away.

HENRY WADSWORTH LONGFELLOW

JOHN SINGER SARGENT: *The Daughters of Edward D. Boit*, 1882

JONATHAN EASTMAN JOHNSON : *The Little Convalescent,* about 1873-1879

16

The Land
of Counterpane

When I was sick and lay a-bed,
I had two pillows at my head,
And all my toys beside me lay
To keep me happy all the day.

And sometimes for an hour or so
I watched my leaden soldiers go,
With different uniforms and drills,
Among the bed-clothes, through the hills;

And sometimes sent my ships in fleets
All up and down among the sheets;
Or brought my trees and houses out,
And planted cities all about.

I was the giant great and still
That sits upon the pillow-hill,
And sees before him, dale and plain,
The pleasant land of counterpane.

ROBERT LOUIS STEVENSON

I Had but Fifty Cents

I took my girl to a fancy ball;
It was a social hop;
We waited till the folks got out,
And the music it did stop.
Then to a restaurant we went,
The best one on the street;
She said she wasn't hungry,
But this is what she eat:
A dozen raw, a plate of slaw,
A chicken and a roast,
Some applesass and sparagrass,
And soft-shell crabs on toast.
A big box stew, and crackers too;
Her appetite was immense!
When she called for pie,
I thought I'd die,
For I had but fifty cents!

ANONYMOUS

PIERRE AUGUSTE RENOIR: *Dance at Bougival*, 1883

Patterns

OSCAR CLAUDE MONET: *La Japonaise*

I walk down the garden paths,
And all the daffodils
Are blowing, and the bright blue squills.
I walk down the patterned garden paths
In my stiff, brocaded gown.
With my powdered hair and jewelled fan,
I too am a rare
Pattern. As I wander down
The garden paths.

AMY LOWELL

A Comparison

Apple blossoms look like snow,
They're different, though.
Snow falls softly, but it brings
Noisy things:
Sleighs and bells, forts and fights,
Cozy nights.

But apple blossoms when they go,
White and slow,
Quiet all the orchard space,
Till the place
Hushed with falling sweetness seems
Filled with dreams.

JOHN FARRAR

SIR LAWRENCE ALMA-TADEMA: *Promise of Spring (Opus CCCIII)*

Auntie's Skirts

Whenever Auntie moves around,
Her dresses make a curious sound;
They trail behind her up the floor,
And trundle after through the door.

ROBERT LOUIS STEVENSON

WILLIAM MORRIS HUNT:
Mrs. Robert C. Winthrop, 1861

EDMUND CHARLES TARBELL
Reverie (Katharine Finn), 1913

Dream Song

Walk with the sun,
Dance at high noon;
And dream when the night falls black;
But when the stars
Vie with the moon,
Then call the lost dream back.

LEWIS ALEXANDER

Little

I am the sister of him
  And he is my brother.
He is too little for us
  To talk to each other.

So every morning I show him
  My doll and my book;
But every morning he still is
  too little to look.

DOROTHY ALDIS

ANONYMOUS: *Thomas Carew Hunt Martin as an Infant, 1857*

PIERRE AUGUSTE RENOIR:
*Children on the Seashore,
Guernsey*

At the Seaside

When I was down beside the sea
A wooden spade they gave to me
To dig the sandy shore.

My holes were empty like a cup,
In every hole the sea came up,
Till it could come no more.

ROBERT LOUIS STEVENSON

My Plan

When I'm a little older
I plan to buy a boat,
And up and down the river
The two of us will float.

I'll have a little cabin
All painted white and red,
With shutters for the window
And curtains for the bed.

I'll have a little cookstove
On which to fry my fishes,
And all the Hudson River
In which to wash my dishes.

MARCHETTE CHUTE

EDMUND CHARLES TARBELL: *Mother and Child in a Boat*, 1892

SAMUEL FINLEY BREESE MORSE: *Little Miss Hone,* 1824

In Honor
of Taffy Topaz

Taffy, the topaz-colored cat,
Thinks now of this and now of that,
But chiefly of his meals.
Asparagus, and cream, and fish
Are objects of his Freudian wish;
What you don't give, he steals.

His gallant heart is strongly stirred
By chink of plate or flight of bird,
He has a plumy tail;
At night he treads of stealthy pad
As merry as Sir Galahad
A-seeking of the Grail.

His amiable amber eyes
Are very friendly, very wise;
Like Buddha, grave and fat,
He sits, regardless of applause,
And thinking, as he kneads his paws,
What fun to be a cat!

CHRISTOPHER MORLEY

ANDREW L. VON WITTKAMP: *Black Cat on a Chair*

Cats

Cats sleep
Anywhere,
Any table,
Any chair,
Top of piano,
Window-ledge,
In the middle,
On the edge,
Open drawer,
Empty shoe,
Anybody's
Lap will do
Fitted in a
Cardboard box,
In the cupboard
With your frocks–
Anywhere!
They don't care!
Cats sleep
Anywhere.

ELEANOR FARJEON

Cat

The black cat yawns,
Opens her jaws,
Stretches her legs,
And shows her claws.

Then she gets up
And stands on four
Long stiff legs
And yawns some more.

She shows her sharp teeth,
She stretches her lip,
Her slice of tongue
Turns up at the tip.

Lifting herself
On delicate toes,
She arches her back
As high as it goes.

She lets herself down
With particular care,
And pads away
With her tail in the air.

MARY BRITTON MILLER

The Cow

The friendly cow all red and white,
    I love with all my heart;
She gives me cream with all her might,
    To eat with apple tart.

She wanders lowing here and there,
    And yet she cannot stray,
All in the pleasant open air,
    The pleasant light of day;

And blown by all the winds that pass
    And wet with all the showers,
She walks among the meadow grass
    And eats the meadow flowers.

ROBERT LOUIS STEVENSON

TOM BROWNE: *Two of Holland's*

JEAN FRANÇOIS MILLET: *Newborn Lamb*

Little Bo-Peep

Little Bo-peep has lost her sheep,
And doesn't know where to find them.
Leave them alone, and they'll come home,
Wagging their tails behind them.

Little Bo-peep fell fast asleep,
And dreamt she heard them bleating.
But when she awoke, she found it a joke,
For they were still a-fleeting.

Then she took up her little crook,
Determined for to find them.
She found them indeed, but it made her heart bleed,
For they'd left all their tails behind them!

ANONYMOUS

A Frisky Lamb

A frisky lamb
And a frisky child
Playing their pranks
In a cowslip meadow:
The sky all blue
And the air all mild
And the fields all sun
And the lanes half shadow.

CHRISTINA ROSSETTI

35

EUGÈNE DELACROIX: *The Royal Tiger,* 1829

The Tyger

Tyger, Tyger burning bright,
In the forests of the night;
What immortal hand or eye
Could name thy fearful symmetry?

In what distant deeps or skies
Burnt the fire of thine eyes?
On what wings dare he aspire?
What the hand dare seize the fire?

And what shoulder & what art
Could twist the sinews of thy heart?
And when thy heart began to beat
What dread hand? & what dread feet?

What the hammer? what the chain,
In what furnace was thy brain?
What the anvil? what dread grasp,
Dare its deadly terrors clasp?

When the stars threw down their spears
And water'd heaven with their tears,
Did he smile his work to see?
Did he who made the Lamb make thee?

Tyger, Tyger burning bright,
In the forests of the night;
What immortal hand or eye
Dare frame thy fearful symmetry?

WILLIAM BLAKE

GEORGE STUBBS: *Lion and Lioness*, 1771

The Lion

The Lion, the Lion, he dwells in the waste,
He has a big head and a very small waist;
But his shoulders are stark, and his jaws
    they are grim,
And a good little child will not play with him.

HILAIRE BELLOC

The Lion

Oh, weep for Mr and Mrs Bryan!
He was eaten by a lion;
Following which, the lion's lioness
Up and swallowed Bryan's Bryaness.

OGDEN NASH

ANONYMOUS: *Lion Rampant*

The Cat and the Moon

The cat went here and there
And the moon spun round like a top
And the nearest kin of the moon,
The creeping cat, looked up.
Black Minnaloushe stared at the moon,
For, wander and wail as he would,
The pure cold light in the sky
Troubled his animal blood.
Minnaloushe runs in the grass
Lifting his delicate feet.
Do you dance, Minnaloushe, do you dance?
When two close kindred meet,
What better than call a dance?
Maybe the moon may learn,
Tired of that courtly fashion
A new dance turn.
Minnaloushe creeps through the grass
From moonlit place to place,
The sacred moon overhead
Has taken a new phase.
Does Minnaloushe know that his pupils
Will pass from change to change,
And that from round to crescent,
From crescent to round they range?
Minnaloushe creeps through the grass
Alone, important and wise,
And lifts to the changing moon
His changing eyes.

W. B. YEATS

EDOUARD MANET: *The Cats' Rendezvous,* 1868

The Cat

You get a wife, you get a house,
Eventually you get a mouse.
You get some words regarding mice,
You get a kitty in a trice.
By two A.M. or thereabout,
The mouse is in, the cat is out.
It dawns upon you, in your cot,
The mouse is silent, the cat is not.
Instead of Pussy, says your spouse,
You should have bought another mouse.

OGDEN NASH

ARTHUR RACKHAM: *"The Cat stole away . . ."* from *Grimm's Fairy Tales*

43

Duck's Ditty

All along the backwater,
   Through the rushes tall,
Ducks are a-dabbling,
   Up tails all!

Ducks' tails, drakes' tails,
   Yellow feet a-quiver,
Yellow bills all out of sight
   Busy in the river!

Slushy green undergrowth
   Where the roaches swim—
Here we keep our larder,
   Cool and full and dim.

Everyone for what he likes!
   We like to be
Heads down, tails up,
   Dabbling free!

High in the blue above
   Swifts whirl and call—
We are down a-dabbling,
   Up tails all!

KENNETH GRAHAME

JOHN FREDERICK HERRICK, SR.: *Ducks and Ducklings*

WINSLOW HOMER: *Leaping Trout (Adirondacks, 1894)*

We Fish

We fish, we fish, we merrily swim,
We care not for friend nor for foe.
Our fins are stout,
Our tails are out,
As through the seas we go.

Fish, fish, we are fish with red gills;
Naught disturbs us, our blood is at zero:
We are bouyant because of our bags,
Being many, each fish is a hero.
We care not what is it, this life

That we follow, this phantom unknown;
To swim, it's exceedingly pleasant—
So swim away, making a foam.
This strange looking thing by our side,
Not for safety, around it we flee:
Its shadow's so shady, that's all—
We only swim under its lee.
And as for the eels there above,
And as for the fowls of the air,
We care not for them nor their ways,
As we cheerily glide afar!

HERMAN MELVILLE

Jamaica Market

Honey, pepper, leaf-green limes
Pagan fruit whose names are rhymes,
Mangoes, breadfruit, ginger-roots,
Granadillas, bamboo-shoots,
Cho-cho, ackees, tangerines,
Lemons, purple Congo-beans,
Sugar, okras, kola-nuts,
Citrons, hairy cocoanuts,
Fish, tobacco, native hats,
Gold bananas, woven mats,
Plantains, wild-thyme, pallid leeks,
Pigeons with their scarlet beaks,
Oranges and saffron yams,
Baskets, ruby guava jams,
Turtles, goat-skins, cinnamon,
Allspice, conch-shells, golden rum.
Black skins, babel—and the sun
That burns all colors into one.

AGNES MAXWELL-HALL

PAUL GAUGUIN: *Where Do We Come From? What Are We? Where Are We Going?* (detail), 1897

ERASTUS SALISBURY FIELD: *The Garden of Eden*

Kindness to Animals

Little children, never give
    Pain to things that feel and live;
Let the gentle robin come
    For the crumbs you save at home—
As his food you throw along
    He'll repay you with a song;
Never hurt the timid hare
    Peeping from her green grass lair,

Let her come and sport and play
    On the lawn at the close of day;
The little lark goes soaring high
    To the bright windows of the sky
Singing as if 'twere always spring,
    And fluttering on an untired wing—
Oh! Let him sing his happy song,
    Nor do these gentle creatures wrong.

ANONYMOUS

49

Where Go the Boats?

Dark brown is the river,
   Golden is the sand.
It flows along for ever,
   With trees on either hand.

Green leaves a-floating,
   Castles of the foam,
Boats of mine a-boating–
   Where will all come home?

On goes the river
   And out past the mill,
Away down the valley,
   Away down the hill.

Away down the river,
   A hundred miles or more,
Other little children
   Shall bring my boats ashore.

ROBERT LOUIS STEVENSON

FRANK WESTON BENSON: *Calm Morning*, 1904

The Pasture

I'm going out to clean the pasture spring;
I'll only stop to rake the leaves away
(And wait to watch the water clear, I may);
I shan't be gone long–You come too.

I'm going out to fetch the little calf
That's standing by the mother. It's so young
It totters when she licks it with her tongue.
I shan't be gone long–You come too.

ROBERT FROST

WINSLOW HOMER: *Boys in a Pasture*, 1874

Childhood Painting Lesson

"Draw me," the cypress said,
"I will hold quite still and bow my head."

"Draw us," the willows cried.
"We will lift our gentle skirts aside."

The poppies called, "We will give you red."
"I will give you silver," the river said.

I recall on this neglected lawn
How the world knelt sweetly to be drawn.

HENRY RAGO

OSCAR CLAUDE MONET: *Poppy Field in a Hollow Near Giverny*

Thanksgiving Day

Over the river and through the woods
  To grandfather's house we go;
    The horse knows the way
    To carry the sleigh
  Through the white and drifted snow.

Over the river and through the wood—
  Oh, how the wind does blow!
    It stings the toes
    And bites the nose,
  As over the ground we go.

Over the river and through the wood,
  To have a first-rate play.
    Hear the bells ring,
    "Ting-a-ling-ding!"
  Hurrah for Thanksgiving Day!

Over the river and through the wood
  Trot fast, my dapple-gray!
    Spring over the ground,
    Like a hunting-hound!
  For this is Thanksgiving Day.

Over the river and through the wood,
  And straight through the barnyard gate.
    We seem to go
    Extremely slow,
  It is so hard to wait!

Over the river and through the wood—
  Now grandmother's cap I spy!
    Hurrah for the fun!
    Is the pudding done?
  Hurrah for the pumpkin-pie!

LYDIA MARIA CHILD

ANONYMOUS: *Musicians in the Snow* (detail), about 1876

The Snow

It sifts from leaden sieves,
It powders all the wood,
It fills with alabaster wool
The wrinkles of the road.

It makes an even face
Of mountain and of plain,
Unbroken forehead from the east
Unto the east again.

It reaches to the fence,
It wraps it, rail by rail,
Till it is lost in fleeces;
It flings a crystal veil

On stump and stack and stern,
The summer's empty room,
Acres of seams where harvests were,
Recordless, but for them.

It ruffles wrists of posts,
As ankles of a queen,
Then stills its artisans like ghosts,
Denying they have been.

EMILY DICKINSON

The Night Was Growing Cold

The night was growing cold
  As she trudged through snow and sleet;
And her nose was long and cold,
  And her shoes were full of feet.

ANONYMOUS

OSCAR CLAUDE MONET: *Boulevard Saint Denis, Argenteuil, in Winter, 1875*

The Way Through the Woods

They shut the way through the woods
Seventy years ago.
Weather and rain have undone it again,
And now you would never know
There was once a road through the woods
Before they planted the trees.
It is underneath the coppice and heath,
And the thin anemones.
Only the keeper sees
That, where the ring-dove broods,
And the badgers roll at ease,
There was once a road through the woods.

Yet, if you enter the woods
Of a summer evening late,
When the night-air cools on the trout-ringed pools
Where the otter whistles his mate,
(They fear not men in the woods,
Because they see so few),
You will hear the beat of a horse's feet,
And the swish of skirt in the dew,
Steadily cantering through
The misty solitudes,
As though they perfectly knew
The old lost road through the woods . . .
But there is no road through the woods!

RUDYARD KIPLING

JACOB ABRAHAM CAMILLE PISSARRO: *Morning Sunlight on the Snow, Eragny-Sur-Epte*, 1895

The Velvet Shoes

Let us walk in the white snow
        In soundless space;
With footsteps quiet and slow,
        At a tranquil pace,
        Under veils of white lace.

I shall go shod in silk,
        And you in wool,
White as a white cow's milk,
        More beautiful
        Than the breast of a gull.

We shall walk through the still town
        In a windless peace;
We shall step upon white down,
        Upon silver fleece,
        Upon softer than these.

We shall walk in velvet shoes:
        Wherever we go
Silence will fall like dews
        On white silence below.
        We shall walk in the snow.

ELINOR WYLIE

60

FREDERICK CHILDE HASSAM: *Boston Common at Twilight*, 1885-1886

Now the Day Is Over

Now the day is over,
  Night is drawing nigh,
Shadows of the evening
  Steal across the sky.

Now the darkness gathers,
  Stars begin to peep,
Birds and beasts and flowers
  Soon will be asleep.

SABINE BARING-GOULD

61

List of Illustrations

Sir Lawrence Alma-Tadema
(Dutch [worked in England], 1836–1912)
Promise of Spring (Opus CCCIII)
Oil on panel, 15 x 7⅞ inches
Bequest of Frances M. Baker
39.94

Anonymous, 19th century American
Lion Rampant
Pen, watercolor, and gouache, 15⅝ x 12¹⁄₁₆ inches
M. and M. Karolik Collection
56.752

Anonymous, 19th century American
Musicians in the Snow (detail), about 1876
Oil on canvas, 30½ x 40½ inches
M. and M. Karolik Collection
47.1219

Anonymous, 19th century American
Thomas Carew Hunt Martin as an Infant, 1857
Watercolor, 7⅛ x 9¹⁄₁₆ inches
M. and M. Karolik Collection
53.2425

Frank Weston Benson (American, 1862–1951)
Calm Morning, 1904
Oil on canvas, 44 x 36 inches
Gift of the Charles A. Coolidge Family
1985.925

Tom Browne (British, 1872–1910)
Two of Holland's
Watercolor, 20¼ x 40⅛ inches
Bequest of John T. Spaulding
1948.879

Mary Stevenson Cassatt (American, 1844–1926)
Ellen Mary in a White Coat, about 1896
Oil on canvas, 34¼ x 24 inches
Anonymous Fractional Gift in Honor of
Ellen Mary Cassatt
1982.630

Eugène Delacroix (French, 1798–1863)
The Royal Tiger, 1829
Lithograph, 19⅜ x 25 inches
Otis Norcross Fund
M25441

Erastus Salisbury Field (American, 1805–1900)
The Garden of Eden
Oil on canvas, 34¾ x 46 inches
Gift of Maxim Karolik for the Karolik Collection of
American Paintings, 1815–1865
48.1027

Paul Gauguin (French, 1848–1903)
*Where Do We Come From? What Are We? Where Are We
Going? (D'où Venons-nous? Que Sommes-nous? Où Allon-
nous? [detail])*, 1897
Oil on canvas, 54¾ x 147½ inches
Tompkins Collection
36.270

Frederick Childe Hassam (American, 1859-1935)
Boston Common at Twilight, 1885–1886
Oil on canvas, 42 x 60 inches
Gift of Miss Maud E. Appleton
31.952

John Frederick Herrick, Sr. (British, 1795–1865)
Ducks and Ducklings
Oil on paperboard, 10¾ x 12 inches
Bequest of Charles Sumner   74.17

Winslow Homer (American, 1836–1910)
Boys in a Pasture, 1874
Oil on canvas, 15¼ x 22½ inches
The Hayden Collection   53.2552

Winslow Homer (American, 1836–1910)
Leaping Trout (Adirondacks, 1894)
Watercolor over graphite on cream woven paper,
13⅞ x 19⅞ inches
William Wilkins Warren Fund
99.24

William Morris Hunt (American, 1824–1879)
Mrs. Robert C. Winthrop (Francis Pickering Adams), 1861
Oil on canvas, 47 x 36 inches
Gift through Miss Clara Bowdoin Winthrop
24.339

Jonathan Eastman Johnson (American, 1824–1906)
The Little Convalescent, about 1873–1879
Oil on academy board, 12¾ x 11 inches
Frederick Brown Fund
40.90

Edouard Manet (French, 1832–1883)
The Cats' Rendezvous, 1868
Lithograph, 17¼ x 13⅛ inches
Gift of W. G. Russell Allen
32.472

Jacob Maris (Dutch, 1837–1899)
Teaching the Dog
Watercolor on paper, 12¾ x 9 inches
Abbot Lawrence Fund
99.3

Jean François Millet (French, 1814–1875)
Newborn Lamb
Pastel and black conté crayon on paper,
15⅞ x 18½ inches. Gift of Quincy Adams Shaw
through Quincy A. Shaw, Jr. and Mrs. Marian
Shaw Haughton
17.1513

Oscar Claude Monet (French, 1840–1926)
Boulevard Saint Denis, Argenteuil, in Winter, 1875
Oil on canvas, 24 x 32⅛ inches
Gift of Richard Saltonstall
1978.633

Oscar Claude Monet (French, 1840–1926)
La Japonaise (Camille Monet in Japanese Costume)
Oil on canvas, 91¼ x 56 inches
1951 Purchase Fund
56.147

Oscar Claude Monet (French, 1840–1926)
Meadow with Poplars
Oil on canvas, 21½ x 25¾ inches
Bequest of David P. Kimball in memory of his wife,
Clara Bertram Kimball
23.505

Oscar Claude Monet (French, 1840–1926)
Poppy Field in a Hollow near Giverny
Oil on canvas, 25⅝ x 32 inches
Juliana Cheney Edwards Collection. Bequest of Robert J.
Edwards in memory of his mother.
25.106

Samuel Finley Breese Morse (American, 1791–1872)
Little Miss Hone, 1824
Oil on panel, 30 x 25 inches
Bequest of Martha C. Karolik for the Karolik Collection
of American Paintings, 1815–1865
48.455

Jacob Abraham Camille Pissarro (Danish [worked in
France], 1830–1903)
Morning Sunlight on the Snow, Eragny-Sur-Epte, 1895
Oil on canvas, 32⅜ x 24¼ inches
John Pickering Lyman Collection. Gift of Theodora Lyman
19.1321

Arthur Rackham (British, 1867–1939)
"The Cat stole away . . ." from
Grimm's Fairy Tales (New York, 1909)
Color illustration 6½ x 5 inches
Gift of Mrs. George Edward Clark
38.860

Pierre Auguste Renoir (French 1841–1919)
Children on the Seashore, Guernsey
Oil on canvas, 36 x 26⅛ inches
Bequest of John T. Spaulding
48.594

Pierre Auguste Renoir (French, 1841–1919)
Dance at Bougival, 1883
Oil on canvas, 71⅝ x 38⅝ inches
Picture Fund
37.375

John Singer Sargent (American, 1856–1925)
The Daughters of Edward D. Boit, 1882
Oil on canvas, 87 x 87 inches
Gift of Mary Louisa Boit, Florence D. Boit,
Jane Hubbard Boit, and Julia Overing Boit, in
memory of their father, Edward Darley Boit
19.124

John Singer Sargent (American, 1856–1925)
Miss Helen Sears (Mrs. J. D. Cameron Bradley), 1895
Oil on canvas, 65¾ x 35¾ inches
Gift of Mrs. J.D. Cameron Bradley
55.1116

George Stubbs (English, 1724–1806)
Lion and Lioness, 1771
Oil on canvas, 40½ x 50¼ inches
M. Theresa B. Hopkins Fund
49.6

Edmund Charles Tarbell (American, 1862–1938)
Mother and Child in a Boat, 1892
Oil on canvas, 30 x 35 inches
Bequest of David P. Kimball in memory of his wife,
Clara Bertram Kimball
23.532

Edmund Charles Tarbell (American, 1862–1938)
Reverie (Katharine Finn), 1913
Oil on canvas, 50¼ x 34¼ inches
Bequest of Georgina S. Cary
33.400

Andrew L. von Wittkamp
(American, 19th century)
Black Cat on a Chair
Oil on canvas, 36 x 29¼ inches
Bequest of Martha C. Karolik for the Karolik
Collection of American Paintings, 1815–1865
48.494

Poetry Acknowledgments

"Little" from *Everything and Anything,* by Dorothy Aldis, copyright © 1925–1927, renewed 1953–1955 by Dorothy Aldis. Reprinted by permission of G.P. Putnam's Sons.

"My Dog" and "My Plan" from *Around and About* by Marchette Chute, copyright © 1957 by E. P. Dutton. Copyright renewed 1984 by Marchette Chute. Reprinted by permission of Elizabeth Roach.

"Cat" by Eleanor Farjeon, copyright © 1957 Eleanor Farjeon, from *The Children's Bells,* copyright © 1957 J.P. Lippincott. Reprinted by permission of Harold Ober Associates Inc.

"A Comparison" by John Farrar, from *Songs for Parents,* 1921 Yale University Press. Reprinted by permission of the Yale University Press.

"The Pasture" by Robert Frost, from *The Poetry of Robert Frost* edited by Edward Connery Lathem. Copyright © 1939, 1967, 1969 by Holt, Rinehart, and Winston. Reprinted by permission of Henry Holt and Company, Inc.

"Patterns" excerpted from the longer work by Amy Lowell, from *The Complete Poetical Works of Amy Lowell.* Copyright © 1953 by Houghton Mifflin Co., renewed 1955 by Houghton Mifflin Co., Brinton P. Roberts, and G. D'Andelot Belin, Esquire. Reprinted by permission.

"The Cat" by Ogden Nash from *Custard and Company,* copyright © 1933 by Ogden Nash and "The Lion" from *Verses from 1929 On,* copyright © 1944 by Ogden Nash. Both reprinted by permission of Little, Brown and Company.

"Childhood Painting Lesson" by Henry Rago. Copyright © 1953, 1981 *The New Yorker Magazine,* Inc. Reprinted by permission.

"The Cat and the Moon" by W. B. Yeats, from *The Poems of W. B. Yeats: A New Edition* edited by Richard J. Finneran, copyright © 1919 by Macmillan Publishing Company, renewed in 1947 by Bertha Georgie Yeats. Reprinted by permission of Macmillan Publishing Company.

About the Editor

Kathryn Sky-Peck's award-winning poetry has been published in the *Antioch Review* and *Tendril,* among other publications. She has studied at the Art Institute of Chicago, and holds a BFA in painting from the University of Illinois, and a graduate degree in poetry from the University of New Hampshire. She has taught university writing courses, poetry workshops, and art at summer enrichment programs for children and is currently with the Museum of Fine Arts, Boston.